Isabel's Secret & Isabel's Fun Fair Fiasco Literature Study Guide

Christian Themes, Literature Focus, Vocabulary, Discussion Questions, and Activities

Jan May

New Millennium Girl Books

Literature Study Guide for

Isabel's Secret and Isabel's Fun Fair Fiasco

Copyright 2023 by Jan May

Education and Language Arts

All rights reserved. No portion of this book may be copied, shared, given away, or reproduced in any manner whatsoever.

ISBN: 978-0-9835281-6-6

Printed in the United States of America

First Edition

Published by New Millennium School Books, 2023

New Millennium School Books

Chapters 1-2
The Secret and Makeover Magic

Literature Focus: Theme

1. A theme is the main idea that runs throughout a story. In this story, the theme is perseverance (not giving up) when things are difficult. One thing you read right away in chapter one is Isabel's motto. What is it?

   _____

   _____

2. Do you have a favorite Bible verse or motto that helps you when things get tough? Write it on the lines below.

   _____

   _____

3. What three things does Isabel do that show perseverance?

   1._____
   2._____
   3._____

Discussion Questions Chapters 1-2

1. What is Isabel's big problem?

   _____

2. How does she think she can solve it?

   _____

   _____

3. Do these things work? _____ Why or why not?
_____
_____

4. Have you ever had a big problem like Isabel? _____
What was it and how did you solve it?
_____
_____

Activity – A life motto is a simple sentence or phrase that sums up what a person or family believes is true, and they try to live by it. Isabel chose the motto she did because she believes in perseverance and not giving up. With the fun bordered paper provided on the next page, write out your life motto or Bible verse that encourages you when things get tough.

My Life Motto

Vocabulary Chapters 1-2
Words in Context

Instructions: Place the correct vocabulary word or phrase into the blank space in the sentence that matches best. Below is the list of words to choose from.

Word List

sheepish	rangeland
dedicated	grimace
essence	catastrophe
chiffon	cuticle cream
concoction	camouflage
scorch	reluctant

1. The gorgeous, lavender-colored summer dress was made of _____ and lace.

2. Jed, the cowboy, took his cattle to the _____ to eat grass and exercise.

3. Dad dressed in _____ when he went hunting so he would blend in with the forest.

4. Jackson, the puppy, was _____ to get wet in the cold water for his bath.

5. Everyone on the basketball team was _____ to working hard and practicing so they could win the championship this year.

6. Jordan gave her mom perfume with the _____ of rose for Mother's Day.

7. Albert was in the basement all night working on his latest _____ for the science fair.

8. All the girls at Merriam's slumber party applied _____ _____ to their fingernails as part of their manicures.

9. Toby smiled a _____ grin after he accidentally spilled water all over the floor.

10. The hurricane caused such a _____ for the people in New Orleans.

11. The patient gave a painful _____ while the nurse examined his wound.

12. The hot midday sun began to _____ the garden, so Mom pulled out the hose and watered it.

Chapters 3-4

The Race and Sleepover

Literature Focus: Character Development

We come to know a character by what they like, do, and say. Make a character web for Isabel and Holly. Even though they are different girls, they each are special in their own way. In the stars below write down all the things that you know about Isabel such as physical features like hair color, her favorite things to do, and what she says.

Make a character web for Holly. Do the same thing as you did for Isabel on the previous page.

Discussion Questions Chapters 3-4

1. Why does Isabel want to beat Kip Johnson?

   _____

   _____

2. Have you ever gotten teased about anything? _____ What was it?

   _____

   _____

3. Did you ever want to win something badly? _____ What was it?

   _____

4. Isabel's parents left to buy a new horse and said they would be back before dark. What happens to prevent them from coming back?

   _____

5. In the kitchen is posted a blizzard emergency list of things to do in case a storm arises. What is on the list?

   _____

   _____

   _____

   _____

   _____

Activity - Make a Safety Storm or Blizzard Sheet

There are some ways you can plan before a disaster occurs. You may never have to use these tips, but you will want to know them just in case.

If you find yourself home alone, take a deep breath and relax! Remember, you are really never alone. The Lord is always with you and can give you wisdom for any situation if you ask.

- Make up a family plan for disasters and post it where every family member can find it.

- Make a blizzard kit ahead of time and keep it where it can be found easily.

    Include:
    o Battery-operated radio with extra batteries.

    o Several flashlights with extra batteries. Avoid candles because of the fire hazard.

- Have an emergency food supply of canned goods, a can opener, and water.

- Designate a spot in the coat closet to keep thermal underwear, hats, and socks.

- Keep board games or arts and crafts for kids handy. A storm could last several days.

- Children may be tempted to go outside but should not go. Blizzard temperatures can be cold enough for frostbite.

- Eat for body heat and jump up and down or move around in the house to stay warm, but do not overexert.

Vocabulary Chapters 3-4
Crossword Puzzle

Instructions: Read the clues below to complete the crossword puzzle. Use the word list for help.

Vocabulary Word List

appaloosa	unpredictable	bask
psyche out	contaminate	acknowledge
recognize	coax	
linoleum	defiant	
podium	influence	
contestant	taunt	

12

Words Across:

2. Any breed of rugged saddle horses developed in western North America and usually having a white or solid-colored coat with small spots

4. To lie or relax happily in a bright and warm place

7. Showing no respect for authority; refusing to obey

8. To get someone to do something by gentle persuasion.

9. Not predictable; not able to be known beforehand.

13. A raised platform for a speaker or orchestra conductor

14. To make dirty, polluted, or not usable by touching or by adding something to

Words Down:

1. someone who takes part in a contest; competitor

3. to make fun of, tease, or challenge in mean language

5. to identify (someone or something) from previous experience or contact with that person or thing

6. to weaken the confidence of, intimidate.

10. the power or invisible action of a thing or person that causes some kind of effect on another

11. to admit or accept the truth

12. a floor covering that is not easily worn out which is made by pressing linseed oil and ground-up wood products onto a canvas backing

Chapters 5-6
Betrayed and The Museum

Literature Focus: Plot

A plot is a road map of where your story is going, with important stops marked along the way. It moves the story from the beginning to the end, with some fun twists along the way.

1. What event is important to the plot and reveals more information about the mystery?

_____

_____

2. There is usually one (or more) GREAT DRAMATIC QUESTION in a novel. This is the unspoken question that every reader is asking in their mind while reading the story. This question MUST be answered by the end of the story. What is the GREATEST DRAMATIC QUESTION in this book?

_____

3. There are several smaller DRAMATIC QUESTIONS along the way. Name one.

_____

_____

4. List one or two questions that you, the reader, would like to see answered by the end of the story.

_____

_____

Discussion Questions Chapters 5-6

1. Why does Isabel feel like her dad is betraying her?

_____

2. Isabel is a tomboy. She likes to do lots of physical activities like catching bugs and getting dirty. Are you more like Isabel or Holly? You are special just the way you are so either answer is the right one! Make a short list of things you like to do.

_____
_____

3. Name four cool artifacts or exhibits the girls see at the museum.

_____
_____
_____
_____

4. What do you think the writing on the pot means?

_____
_____

5. Why does Isabel feel "creepy"?

_____
_____

Activity - Make Friendship Bracelets

- 1 cup of salt
- 2 cups white flour
- up to 1 cup of warm water
- food coloring
- elastic string
- skewer to poke holes in beads

Mix the salt and flour together in a bowl. Pour in some of the warm water until it thickens the mixture. (You may not need the full cup of water.) Pour it in slowly until the consistency is like play dough.

Separate the dough into four-to-six equal pieces. Add a few drops of food coloring to each of the pieces. For fun: swirl together two colors for two of the portions. Knead the dough for a few minutes, mixing the colors in until smooth.

Roll small pieces as large as you want the beads to be in the palms of your hands to form balls. Mix a few colors together to form a swirl effect. You can also form squares or cut out different small shapes.

Make a large hole in the center of each bead with a wooden chopstick or skewer. The hole will shrink while baking.

Line a cookie sheet with parchment paper and bake beads at 200⁰ for 3-4 hours until they are dry.

Thread the beads with elastic string and tie a knot at the ends. Share one with your BFF. Share one with someone who needs a friend!

Vocabulary Words Chapters 5-6

Word Search

Instructions: Circle the eleven vocabulary words in the puzzle below. (See word list that follows.) Words can be found vertically, horizontally, or diagonally. When you have finished, look up the definitions and write them next to the words. Happy searching!

```
P V S C V N F K E K U D P F Y
T A A A O Q U D Z D V P R O Y
U O P A N I T D N F G S W O P
N O T O P T N U I Q E Z W L O
E Y M E O A I C R Z W M L S R
A A V D M S T C I Q F B J G T
R C P O I P E O I D U O H O A
T O I S J N O Z S P E O P L L
H I K M L W K L P A A N I D T
H N E C J A V P E V U T C S H
M C S N A X G H V A Q R I E E
U I P J M O N O E A R E U O A
E D E R B I G Q Z S E S B S N
C E A Y L T U R A U Q A V Y Z
Z S K T E G H L D E G R D U J
```

Word List - Write out the Definitions

COINCIDENCE -
_____
_____

PIKES PEAK -
_____
_____

TOTEM POLE -
_____
_____

AMBLE -
_____
_____

UNEARTH -
_____
_____

TURQUOISE -
_____
_____

PAPOOSE -
_____
_____

ANTICIPATION -
_____
_____

PORTAL -
_____
_____

FOOLS GOLD -
_____
_____

APATOSAURUS -
_____
_____

Chapters 7-8
Camp Tialocka and Jason Twofeathers

Literature Focus: Sensory Setting

A setting is a place where the story happens and the time in history. In these chapters, the setting is Camp Tialocka in Colorado Springs, Colorado.

The *sensory* setting is when an author uses all five senses to describe the setting so that the readers will not just read the story but experience it through their senses.

The five senses are **sight**, **sound**, **smell**, **taste**, and **touch**. For each of the sentences below, identify which of the five senses the author used to describe the setting.

1. The other girls on the bus sang silly camp songs all the way to Camp Tialocka. _____

2. Twelve rustic pine cabins sat on the bank of a shimmering lake. _____

3. "These horses are smelly," said Amanda, holding her nose. _____

4. Yellow and blue butterflies fluttered around the bushes. _____

5. A redwing blackbird called out, and the locusts were starting to hum. _____

6. The hot summer heat made her legs stick to the saddle. _____

Discussion Questions Chapters 7-8

1. What changes Isabel's mind about liking girly things?
   _____

2. Why are Amanda Parkington's friends called the "Snob Mob"?
   _____

3. Name some of Isabel's activities at camp.
   _____
   _____
   _____

4. Have you ever gone to summer camp? What were some of your favorite activities there? Or if you have never attended camp, what would you LIKE to do there?
   _____
   _____
   _____

Vocabulary Chapters 7-8

Words in Context

Word List

irritate	notorious	French manicure
elaborate	industrious	American paint horse
canter	rustic	sympathetic
obvious	dipper bird	suspicious

Instructions: Place the vocabulary word or phrase in the blank space in the sentence that matches it best. Choose from the words listed in the word box above.

1. Madeline was acting very _____ after the pie in the window went missing.

2. The cabin that Tiffany and Leanne stayed in over the summer was very _____ inside.

3. While Ben was trying to concentrate, David began to _____ Ben with his constant whistling and humming.

4. William was _____ towards his sister Lacey when she fell and scraped her knee.

5. Jesse James was a _____ outlaw from the Wild West.

6. On the way back from the fields, Rocket, the mustang, began to _____.

7. It was very _____ that the girl scouts were getting tired from the long hike.

8. All the bridesmaids got a _____ and a makeover before the wedding.

9. Because Emma was so _____ at work, her boss gave her a raise.

10. On the camping trip Mark spotted a _____ diving into the river.

11. The teacher asked Kimberly to _____ more about her school project.

12. Mocha, an _____ horse, has a colorful, one-of-a-kind, white-and-brown coat that looks like splatter marks.

Chapters 9-10
Powwow and Dresses with Bells

Social Studies Focus: What is a Powwow?

A modern-day powwow is a celebration where Native American people gather and enjoy a festival with dancing, singing, and honoring the traditions of their culture. They wear traditional clothing called "regalia," like buckskin pants and dresses. Modern-day powwows may last from one to four days and draw people from 100 miles around. Some offer contests in Native American singing and dancing. One fun dance is the Bear Dance.

Discussion Questions Chapters 9-10

1. What special event does Isabel want to participate in at the powwow?

_____

2. What secret does she discover while she's there?

_____

3. Jason gives Isabel a new name. What is it?

_____

4. What special gift does Isabel receive from her Native American grandma? _____

5. Have you ever received a special gift from your grandma that was hers when she was a little girl? What was it? If not, what would you like her to give you?_____

_____

Activity - Make a Name Decoration for your Bedroom

Names have special meanings given to us by our parents. During Bible times, people named babies for important events or what they believed God for. Make a special nameplate decoration for your bedroom. Make them with your sister or best friend. Include fun photos of yourselves or special mementos.

You will need:

1. Large and small stickers
2. Wall-art decals
3. Small paper plates in variety of colors
4. Black magic marker
5. Alphabet stickers
6. Puff paints or puff glue
7. Wide ribbon (2-3 inch wide); 3 yards long for each nameplate
8. Butterflies, plastic or sticker
9. Fun photos if desired

- Choose the type and number of plates you want to use. Lay them out on the table or floor so you can see what they look like together. In the example, we chose a flowered plate to glue on top of a pink one in an alternating pattern.

- Cut out the letters and pictures of the stickers you want to use, but don't peel and stick them yet (in case you want to change them around). Arrange them on the plates first to see how they look.

- On the top plate, use the alphabet stickers and spell your name. Then decorate around it with stickers or glitter glue.

- On the next plate, write what your name means, or write a Bible verse and decorate the plate.

- Use large stickers that are sold for wall art to put in the middle of the next plate. Or draw a special word in glitter paint.

- Roll out the ribbon and lay the plates on top of it in the order. Leave about 2 inches between each plate and 4 extra inches on top. Use a hot glue gun to apply a couple lines of glue right in the middle of the BACK of the plate. Be careful, it's hot! (Have a parent supervise.) Then flip the plate over and attach it to the ribbon. We used the glue bottle to press it firmly in place because it was hot. Do this with all the plates.

- Tie a bow with the extra ribbon and attach it above the top plate on the ribbon with hot glue.

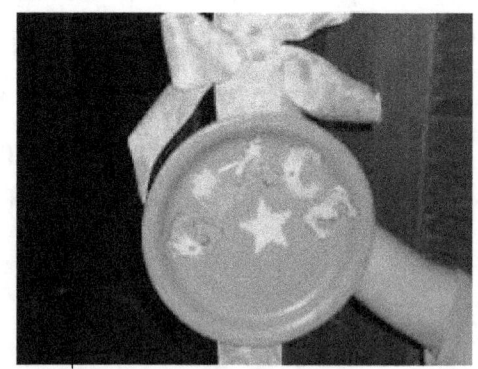

Chapters 9-10 Vocabulary Words
Crossword Puzzle

Directions-On the next several pages find the clues to fill in the crossword puzzle.

Vocabulary Word List

conjure	eagle formation	powwow
Sacajawea	muse	torrent
gold rush	reservation	prospector
Sitting Bull	fry bread	saunter
mustang		

Crossword Puzzle Clues Chapters 9-10

Across

4. rapid movement of people to California in 1848-1849 seeking treasure
5. to think about something carefully for a long time
6. large amount of water that moves very quickly in one direction
11. chosen area of land for Native Americans to live on and taken care of by a Native American tribe under the US Bureau of Indian Affairs me
12. to create or imagine something
13. North American Indian ceremony involving feasting, singing, and dancing

Down

1. flat dough fried or deep-fried in oil, shortening, or lard
2. person who searches for precious minerals and metals
3. small and strong wild horse of western North America
7. group standing in the shape of an eagle
8. to walk along in a slow and relaxed manner
9. Native American leader of the Sioux tribe in the late nineteenth century. He was a chief and medicine man when the Sioux took up arms against the settlers in the northern Great Plains and against United States Army troops
10. young Native American woman who guided Meriwether Lewis and William Clark on their expedition to explore territory gained through the Louisiana Purchase

Vocabulary Crossword Puzzle Chapters 9-10

Chapters 11-12

The Letter and The Reporter

Social Studies Focus

Native Americans told stories about their families and passed them on to each generation. They loved telling stories with good life lessons. It was a way to remember family history. We have books today like the Bible and *Aesop's Fables* that teach us good life lessons.

1. Grandmother Tabitha makes Isabel a special item for story-telling time. What is it?

   _____

2. Do you have a special blanket or tent that you like to sit under when you read books or tell stories to your siblings? Where is it?

   _____
   _____

Discussion Questions Chapters 11-12

1. Native American beliefs differ from Christianity. They believe in a Creator as we do, but we also believe in God's Son, Jesus. That's a big difference! Isabel respects their faith even though she doesn't agree with it. Do you have friends who have different beliefs than you do? If so, write down several ways you can share your faith with them.

_____
_____
_____
_____
_____

2. Native Americans also respect the earth by taking good care of it and only killing animals when their people are hungry. In what ways do you help take care of the earth that God gave us? Recycling or throwing away your trash after a picnic are some ideas.

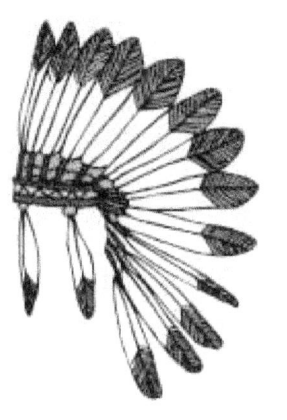

_____
_____
_____
_____
_____

3. Native Americans love to tell stories about animals to help them learn good life lessons. When Grandmother Tabitha told her story about Ben Sawee, the eagle, God helped Isabel see that He was going to help with her problem. Have you ever read stories about life lessons like *Aesop's Fables* or Bible parables that gave you wisdom for a problem? If so, write down several titles of your favorite ones.

_____
_____
_____
_____

Activity – Make Chocolaty-Peanut Butter Native American Teepee Treats

Isabel makes these for a special Native American friend in the book, *Isabel's Secret*.

You will need:

Smooth peanut butter
16-oz bag chocolate chips
Candy corn and pumpkins
Pretzel sticks-small bag
12 pointy ice-cream cones

1. Microwave chocolate chips on high for 1 minute at a time until melted. Don't over-melt! Stir each time.

2. Using a butter knife, coat the inside of each cone **thickly** with peanut butter.

3. With a spoon, drizzle a layer of melted chocolate over the peanut butter inside the cone.

4. Use scissors to cut 1 ½ inches off the top of the cone. Hold the cone on its side and be careful not to let the chocolate drip out.

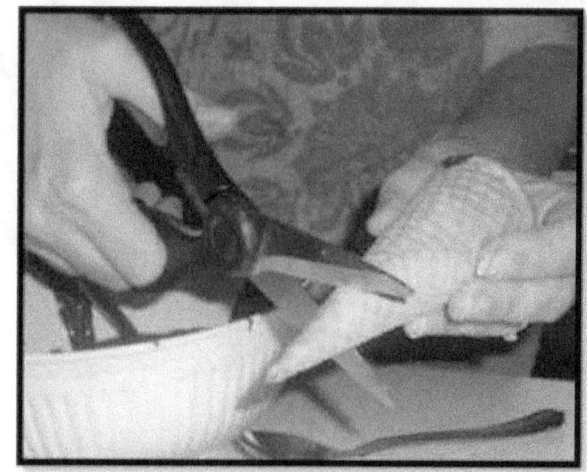

5. Hold the cone on its side and push 3 pretzel sticks in the top.

6. Lay the teepees on their sides on a tray lined with wax paper. Put into the freezer for 15-20 minutes or until the chocolate is solid.

7. With the remainder of the melted chocolate, coat the bottom with a line of chocolate and use that as "glue" for the candy corn.

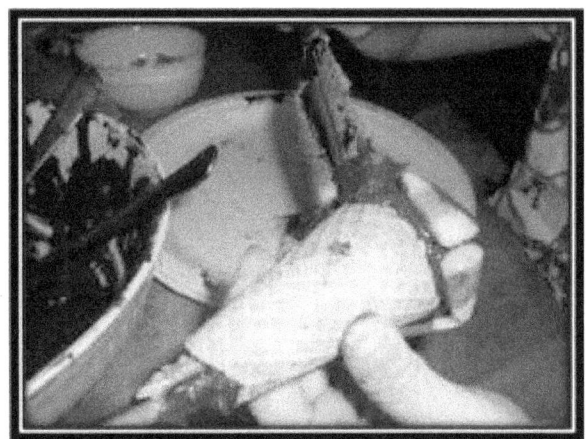

8. For something different, you can cut up the candy corn with a knife to place on top of the chocolate

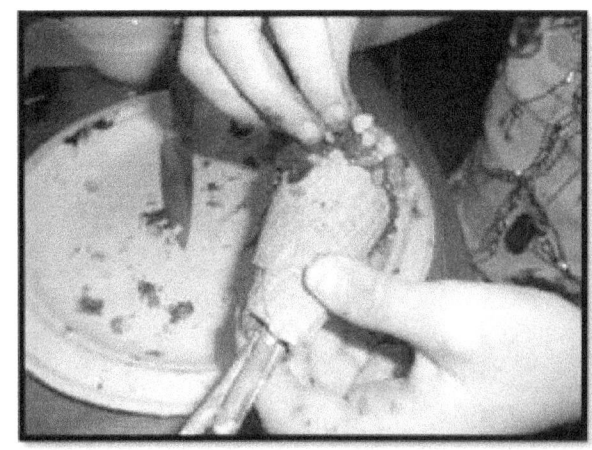

9. "Glue" candy corn in the middle with melted chocolate the same way or use your own designs.

Chapters 11-12 Vocabulary

Word Search

Instructions: Circle eleven vocabulary words in the puzzle below. (See word list that follows.) Words can be found vertically, horizontally, or diagonally. When you have finished, look up the definitions and write them next to the words. Happy searching!

Word List-Write out the Definitions

GIDDY-
_____
_____

HERITAGE -
_____
_____

DOCUMENTARY -
_____
_____

PERSONALITY -
_____
_____

INSTRUCTION -
_____
_____

SOLUTION -
_____
_____

LAMENT -
_____
_____

GOVERNMENT GRANT -
_____
_____

LANYARD -
_____
_____

SLATHER -
_____
_____

PUBLICITY -
_____
_____

About the Author

Jan May loved homeschooling her two children through high school. Whether it was crafting an ocean diorama or bubble painting, hands-on education was always at the forefront of her curriculum. She is the author of the New Millennium Girl Series, Christian novels for girls that inspire faith. She also authored the *Creative Writing Made Easy* series that engages even the most reluctant writers. All the books are filled with fun activities involving each type of learner: visual, auditory, and kinesthetic—perfect for craft-loving girls! Having been a creative writing teacher for over fifteen years, she believes that given the right tools, every child can learn to write and love it!

Visit her website for fun crafts, downloads, and activities. Watch for her online teaching schedule—leading students and teens in a fun and engaging writing experience.

If you enjoyed this book, you might also enjoy:

Isabel's Book #2 - Isabel's Fun Fair Fiasco

Princess and Frog, Write a Fairytale Adventure

Callie's Contest of Courage

Callie's Literature Study Guide

Order this book and more at www.NewMillenniumGirlBooks.com

Isabel's Secret Study Guide Answer Key

Literature Questions Chapters 1-2

1. "Winners never quit, and quitters never win, for I serve the mighty God that lives deep within!"

2. Answers will vary.

3. Any three of these:

    a She tries wearing a dress even though she doesn't like it.
    b She asks Holly for a makeover.
    c She encourages herself with her motto after she falls down the stairs in her dress.
    d She keeps practicing racing fast to beat Kip Johnson.

Discussion Questions

1) Gran thinks she is a tomboy and needs to go to a girl's school in Boston.
2) Holly giving her a makeover.
3) No, she trips on the stairs and tears her dress.
4) Answers will vary.

Vocabulary Chapters 1-2

1. Chiffon
2. Rangeland
3. Camouflage

4. Reluctant
5. Dedicated
6. Essence
7. Concoctions
8. Cuticle Cream
9. Sheepish
10. Catastrophe
11. Grimace
12. Scorch

Discussion Questions Chapters 3-4

1. Because he keeps teasing her that boys are better riders than girls.
2. Answers will vary.
3. Answers will vary.
4. Blizzard
5. Roll towels underneath the windows and doors, fill a pan of water for drinking, get out flashlights in case of a power outage, put on thermal underwear, drip water in faucets in case pipes freeze, and listen to the weather station on the radio.

Crossword Answers Chapters 3-4

Across

2. Appaloosa
4. Bask
7. Defiant
8. Coax
9. Unpredictable

13. Podium

14. Contaminate

Answers Down

1. Contestant

3. Taunt

5. Recognize

6. Psyche out

10. Influence

11. Acknowledge

12. Linoleum

Literature Questions Chapters 5-6

1. Finding the clay pot with the writing on it.
2. What is Gran's secret?
3. Will Isabel go to Gran's school in Boston?
4. Answers will vary.

Discussion Questions Chapters 5-6

1. Dad is sending Isabel to "girl" camp.
2. Answers will vary. (Holly or Isabel)
3. Teepee, cradleboard, jewelry, stuffed eagles and bears, photos, pipes

4. Accept any reasonable answer.
5. She doesn't know what it all means.

Vocabulary Word Search Answers Chapters 5-6

Literature Questions Chapters 7-8

1. sound
2. sight
3. smell
4. sight
5. sound

6. touch

Discussion Questions Chapter 7-8

1. She made a pretty bracelet.

2. Because they were proud and thought they were better than all the other girls.

3. Archery, wilderness skills, jewelry making, and horse games.

4. Answers will vary

Vocabulary Chapters 7-8

1. Suspicious
2. Rustic
3. Irritate
4. Sympathetic
5. Notorious
6. Canter
7. Obvious
8. French manicure
9. Industrious
10. Dipper Bird
11. Elaborate
12. Appaloosa

Discussion Questions Chapters 9-10

1. Horse Competitions
2. She is part Native American.
3. Mourning Dove
4. Necklace
5. Answers will vary.

Vocabulary Crossword Puzzle Answers

Social Studies Focus Questions Chapters 11-12

1. Story Blanket
2. Answers will vary.

Discussion Questions Chapters 11-12

1.-3. Answers will vary.

Word Search Chapters 11-12

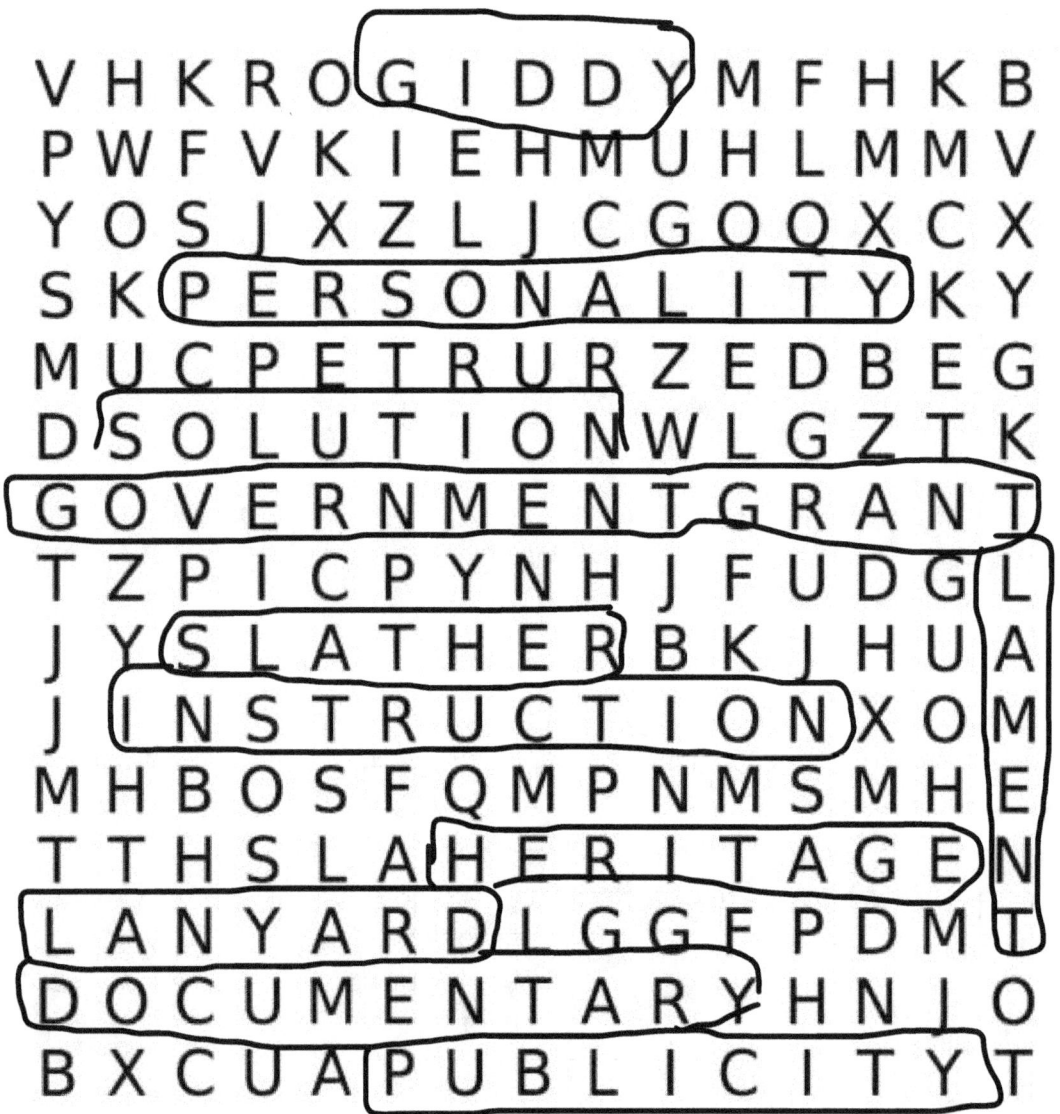

48

Isabel's Fun Fair Fiasco Literature Study Guide

Jan May

New Millennium Girl Books

Chapters 1-2
Little Chaps Rodeo & Pinecone Turkeys

Literature Focus

1. Onomatopoeia is a fun literary tool when a word's pronunciation imitates its sound. Some examples are Boom! Purr! Swish!

There are three examples of this in chapter one. Can you find the three Onomatopoeia words and write them down?

1._____

2._____

3._____

Below is a short list of Onomatopoeia words. Circle two words in the list and write a sentence with Isabel, Holly, or Starlight.

Arf	Blab	Chatter	Jingle
Achoo	Blurt	Swish	Giggle
Buzz	Clip Clop	Boom	Sizzle

1._____

2._____

Social Studies Focus

A Native American Reservation is a large plot of land that the United States government gave the Native Americans in the 1800s to live on. Much of the land was in poor condition, and far from jobs and economic opportunities. Many people feel that it was unfair of the U.S. government to do this. Over the years many reservations became a place of poverty. There are 326 Reservations in the U.S. today. Twenty-five states have reservations. California has the most reservations at 121.

1. Have you ever visited a Native American Reservation? If so, tell about your experience:

_____
_____
_____
_____

2. Have you ever been to a festival where you celebrated your national heritage? If so, what were some of the things you did?

_____
_____

Rodeos are competitions that feature cowboy skills like horse riding, roping, and cattle wrangling. There are thousands of rodeos worldwide every year. Houston, Texas has the world's largest rodeo for 20 days with over 2 million people in attendance. It consists of bull riding, horse racing, rope competitions, parades, BBQ contests, pig racing, concerts, horse trail rides, and much more!

3. What surprise event happened at the Little Chaps rodeo?
_____
_____
_____

4. What happened when a horse spooked near Isabel?
_____
_____
_____

5. Have you ever been to a rodeo? If so, describe it here. Also, if you have never been to one, would you like to?
_____
_____
_____

Make Pinecone Turkey Place Card Holders

For Each Turkey you will Need:

- 1 Large pinecone
- 2 orange and 2 red pipe cleaners
- 1 piece of yellow construction paper
- 1 piece of red construction paper
- Gold glitter glue or puff paint-small bottle
- Puff paint for eyes, black or other colors
- Glue stick, liquid glue, and hot glue
- **Use hot glue with caution. It could cause burns. Have adults do that part!

Take an orange pipe cleaner and bend it in a little W shape. This will be the three toes and feet of the turkey. Cross the ends over and twist them together from the cross over to the top-this is the legs.

Close the gap on the toes together and bend the tall part of the legs down and twist again until you get feet like in the photo below. Turn the pinecone over and hot glue the feet inside the cone. Be very CAREFUL- hot glue guns can cause burns! Let an adult do this part!

Take a red pipe cleaner and bend it in half. Bend that in half again. Make a small loop at the bent end. Leaving a small hole in that end, twist the rest all the way to the end. This will be the neck. The hole will be the head.

Cut an inch piece of orange pipe cleaner and bend it in half. This will be the beak. Dot the center of the head, where there is a hole with liquid glue-DO NOT USE HOT GLUE-and insert the beak. Hot glue the neck in the middle of the pinecone near the front. Make eyes with black puff paint or use any color you have and when it dries, use a black magic marker and color the eyes black.

Cut a yellow piece of construction paper in half longwise. Measure and cut one – one-inch strip of orange construction paper 10 inches long. Cut another one in red the same size but use scrapbooking scissors to get a jagged edge across one long side. Using a glue stick, glue the red strip near the bottom onto the yellow piece and the orange one near the top leaving, yellow stripes in between.

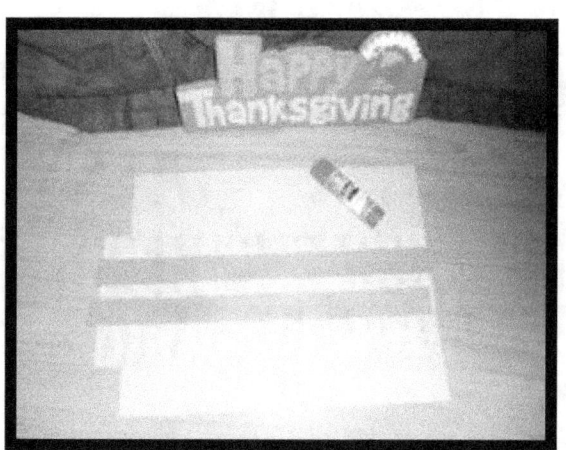

With a tube of glitter paint, make curly cues on all the yellow parts. Take a napkin and blot the glitter and spread it around a bit.

After the glitter paint dries, fold the end about one inch and bend it back and forth making an accordion fold.

Gather the ends of the accordion tail and staple the end near the red stripe. Using a hot glue gun, glue it onto the back of the pinecone. Lay the tail flat on the workspace, add hot glue to it first and press the turkey on top of it. Stand the turkey upright and reinforce the tail with hot glue again.

Take 4 inches of red pipe cleaner and shape it like a hook for the wattle. Bend the piece up an inch to make the bottom a little thicker than the top. Twist it together. Hook and glue it around the beak. Measure 2 x 4-inch pieces of yellow or orange construction paper. Write the name of your guest across the top, and then slip it into the back of the pinecone. (See picture at beginning of craft.) Use for place cards for Thanksgiving Dinner.

Happy Thanksgiving!

Chapters 3-4
Family & Christmas Surprise

Social Studies Focus:

Thanksgiving is a special holiday where friends and family gather together for a special meal. People want to give thanks to God and remember how He watched over them to establish our nation many years ago.

During the first Thanksgiving, the Native Americans brought 5 deer and 50 people. It had been a long hard winter the year before the first Thanksgiving when sickness abounded, and many pilgrims died. By the time the next year rolled around an Indian brave named Squanto taught the pilgrims how to farm and fish in the new land of America. Have you ever moved somewhere new and felt all alone? Was there a special friend like Squanto that wanted to be your friend?

1. Many people want to reach out to others around them and share God's love. Do you ever do special things when you hear about others who have needs? What did Isabel and Holly do?

_____

_____

2. When the Morningsky family arrived at Grandmother Tabitha's house Jason Twofeathers was there cooking something. What was it?

_____

3. A mother with three small children smelled the deer cooking and came over. What did they say to her?

_____

4. How can you help someone in need? Jesus said, *"Truly I tell you, whatever you did for one of the least of these brothers and sisters of mine, you did for me." (Matthew* **25:40**)

Write a name next to each item below:

Take soup to a sick friend or neighbor _____

Give gently used clothes or toys to _____

Help someone clean their house _____

Help babysit for a busy mom _____

Rake leaves or shovel snow for an elderly neighbor _____

Other

_____
_____
_____

Activity

Make Isabel's Yummy Cranberry Gelato

No cooking!

1 - 14 oz sweet, condensed milk

¼ c lemon juice

1 - 20 oz can of crushed pineapple with juice

1 - 16 oz can whole cranberries

1 - 12 oz container of whipped topping

½ cup chopped pecans

Small paper cups

Spray paper cups with a light coating of cooking spray to help them easily slide out. Mix all ingredients together then pour into paper cups and place a pop cycle stick in the middle. Freeze for 1-2 hours until frozen. Take out 10-15 minutes before serving. Slide-out of cups.

Chapters 3-4

Vocabulary Words - Matching

Draw a line matching the vocabulary word on the left with its definition on the right.

Grimace	Plentiful
Generous	Attack
Brimmed	Painful expression
Ghost town	Forever
Abandoned	Overflowing
Eternity	A town where no one lives
Buckskin	To keep trying
Raiding	Animal skin clothing
Determined	To leave

Play Vocabulary Mash-up-Mania by writing a funny sentence on the lines on the next several pages using one word from each column in any order.

Vocab Words	Animals	Objects
Ghost town	Ostrich	shack
Abandoned	Platypus	mittens
Eternity	Raccoon	deer meat

62

Buckskin	Mouse	wildflowers
Raiding	Kangaroo	cranberry gelato
Determined	Lion	purple yarn
Grimaced	Zebra	tree house
Generous	Spider	cake balls
Brimmed	Buzzard	BBQ Pork chops

1. _____
_____
_____

2. _____
_____
_____

3. _____
_____
_____

4. _____
_____
_____

5._____
_____
_____

6._____
_____
_____

7._____
_____
_____

8._____
_____
_____

9._____
_____
_____

Chapters 5-6

Spring Fling Wing Ding & The Horse Whisperer

Literature Focus - An Alliteration is a repetition of the same letter or sound at the beginning of several words next to each other.

Can you name the 4 Alliterations mentioned in these 2 chapters?

_____
_____
_____
_____

Discussion Questions

1. Why did Isabel's mom want to have the Spring Fling Wing Ding?

_____

2. Mom postponed something important to Isabel. What was it?

_____
_____

3. Holly made something special for the Wing Ding. What was it?

_____

4. Amanda Parkington wanted Isabel's mom to cater her birthday party. Did this make Isabel happy? Why or why not?

_____
_____

5. Who was the horse whisperer?
_____
_____

Activity-Make Gracie Lou's Banana-Bandana Punch

Ingredients

4 ripe bananas

2 cups white sugar

3 cups water

1 (46 oz) can of pineapple juice

2 (12 oz cans) frozen orange juice concentrate

1 (12 oz can) frozen lemonade concentrate

3 cups water

3 liters of ginger ale

Directions Combine peeled bananas, sugar, and 3 cups of water in a blender. Blend until smooth. Then blend in the orange juice concentrate, lemonade concentrate, and 3 cups of water. Pour mixture into a large bowl and stir in pineapple juice. Divide into 3 plastic containers and freeze until solid. (Rinsed and cleaned out plastic milk jugs works well!)

Remove jugs from the freezer 4 hours before serving. Using one jug at a time, pour the slushy contents into a large pitcher or punch bowl and add 1 liter of ginger ale for each gallon. Stir. Enjoy! ☺

Chapters 5-6 Crossword Puzzle - Vocabulary Words on Next Pages

Across

4. small hills at the bottom of mountains

5. a fun gathering to help raise money for a good cause

7. Native American word for leader

8. to put off doing something until another time

10. a person who trains horses with gentleness and respect

Down

1. respect or fond approval

2. many balloons tied together to form a tower

3. people who watch or listen to an event

6. delicious

9. the date of an event that happened the previous year

10. the art or practice of riding horses

Vocabulary Words

*Match the words to the crossword puzzle.
Then write the definitions next to the word.*

Potential

_____

Fundraiser

_____

Audience

_____

Postpone

_____

Balloon Tower

_____

Catering

_____

Admiration

_____

Foothills

_____

Anniversary

_____

Itancan

___

Horsemanship

___

Transformed

___

Scrumptious

___

Horse Whisper

___

Chapters 7-8
Mourning Dove & Patterson's Curse

Literature Focus-Similes

A **simile** is a figure of speech that compares one thing to another using "like" or "as" to give a better picture of what something is like. There are many **similes** in this chapter. Do you remember any of them? Below are four of them. Look on the page number and finish the sentence.

Pg. 76 Isabel heard Grandmother Biltmore's booming voice like
_____.

Pg. 72 Limo drove up the driveway like
_____.

Pg. 72 Surrounded Amanda like
_____.

Pg. 80 It was as if
_____.

Discussion Questions

1. Why did Jason say that names are important? Do you agree? Why or why not?

_____

_____

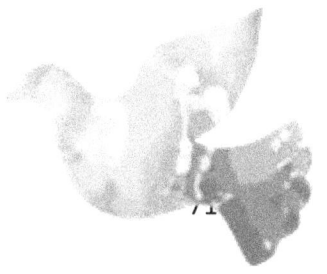

2. What did Jason do at the creek?

_____

_____

3. Why was Isabel upset when Amanda drove up?

_____

_____

4. Who else came that Isabel was not happy about?

_____

_____

5. What is Patterson's Curse?

_____

_____

6. Dad said they hadn't had that plant on the ranch in fifteen years. What do you think? Did someone poison the horses on purpose? Why or why not?

_____

_____

Activity

Grow your name with radish seeds.

Begin by soaking 2 packages of radish seeds overnight. Find a clear patch of soil in your garden free from rocks, grass, and weeds. With a shovel, turn the soil over to loosen it. With a stick write your name in capital letters about 1 inch deep in the dirt leaving 2-3 inches between the letters. Sprinkle the radish seeds in the letters. Then cover lightly with soil and pat down gently. Water every day if it's hot and doesn't rain. Radishes will grow to maturity in 2-3 weeks. For something extra decorate with garden ornaments like butterflies or birdfeeders.

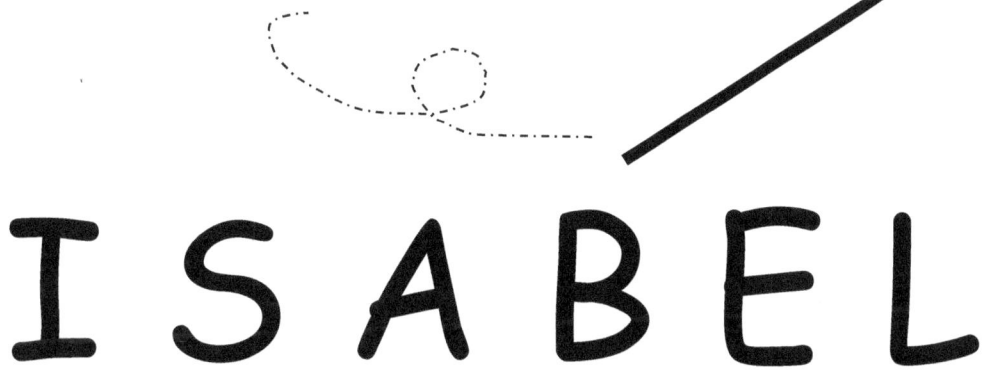

ISABEL

Chapters 7-8 Vocabulary

Words in Context

Instructions: Place the vocabulary word or phrase in the blank space in the sentence that matches it best. Choose from the words listed in the word box below.

saddlebag	destiny	demonstration
limousine	compliment	emerge
chauffer	Paterson's curse	vigorous

1. Jason reached into his _____ and pulled out a packet of radish seeds.

2. Izzy's mom showed the audience how to mix up different recipes during her food _____.

3. Holly gave Isabel a _____ about her new French braids.

4. The _____ drove Amanda and her mom to the mall.

5. Salvation Jane is another name for _____ which is a poisonous plant for animals.

6. Isabel's parents believed that her _____ was to be a strong Christian girl.

7. Isabel and Jason watched as the butterfly _____ from its cocoon.

8. Holly and her family road in a _____ on their way to the airport.

9. Starlight was a _____ horse who could run and jump and never get tired.

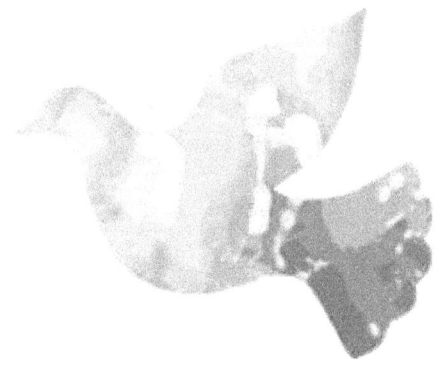

Chapters 9-10
Chunky Nutter Bars & Pink Pony Palace

Literature Focus

A genre is a specific type of music, movie, or book. There are many genres such as fantasy, comedy, science fiction, and action-adventure just to name a few. These Isabel books are called mystery fiction.

In mysteries, there are some common elements.

1. A crime to solve
2. The main character who acts like a detective finding clues and putting them together like a puzzle
3. A group of suspects each having a motive to commit the crime
4. A feeling of suspense throughout the book

Fill in the blank about *Isabel's Fun Fair Fiasco* below:

1. What was the crime?

2. Who is the main character who acts like a detective? _____

3. Who are the suspects in this story? And what are their possible motives? Fill in the blanks on the next page to answer this question.

Suspects	Motives
_____	_____
_____	_____
_____	_____
_____	_____

List the Clues Found in these Chapters:

1._____

2._____

3._____

4._____

Sometimes weather creates a sad or suspenseful mood. When Isabel found out about the horses what was the weather like?

_____

_____

Discussion Questions

1. What did Isabel find in Starlight's stall?

_____

_____

2 Why did Isabel accuse Bo, the ranch hand?

_____

_____

3. Where did they move the horse training? Why was Isabel so upset?

_____

_____

4. Isabel helped her mom prepare food for Amanda's party. Have you ever helped prepare for a party? What did you do?

_____

_____

5. Isabel was worried all day about something. What was it?

_____

_____

Chapters 9-10

Vocabulary Words – Word Search

```
M T G S D M Q I Q S L X P Q A S P D
G W H E S E N N U P Q P F B J U G E
Z J R D C L V V Z Y U K M L P S A M
D S E B R O M E P F H G M W E P R O
K U V R U A I S L D E Z G U R I G N
T S O F T T X T Y O R U Q B S C A S
A P L F I H U I B T P L I C U I N T
F E T D N S W G Q H E M X D A O T R
X C I R I O Z A M U Q D E U D U U A
O T N B Z M T T O W Q J A N E S A T
F N G S E E D E R N K C V O T R N E
S Y M P A T H E T I C R X L B I B S
```

Find the following words in the puzzle.
Words are hidden → ↓ and ↘.

DEMONSTRATE
DEVELOPMENT
GARGANTUAN
INVESTIGATE

LOATHSOME
PERSUADE
REVOLTING
SCRUTINIZE

SUSPECT
SUSPICIOUS
SYMPATHETIC

Vocabulary Word List- Look up the definitions and write them next to the words.

1) DEMONSTRATE -
_____
_____

2) DEVELOPMENT -
_____
_____

3) GARGANTUAN -
_____
_____

4) INVESTIGATE-
_____
_____

5) LOATHSOME -
_____
_____

6) PERSUADE -
_____
_____

7) REVOLTING -

8) SCRUTINIZE -

9) SUSPECT -

10) SUSPICIOUS -

11) SYMPATHETIC -

Activity – Make a Marbled Horse Painting

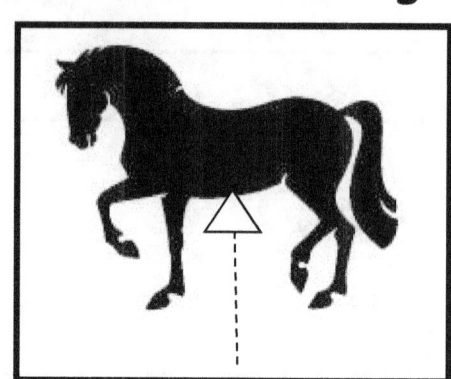

You will need:

- Shallow shirt box – 9 x 11
- Acrylic paints in 3-4 favorite colors
- Marbles
- White sheet of plain 8.5 x 11 paper
- Pink, or purple piece of construction paper

Directions - IMPORTANT: Read all instructions before you begin!

- Tape down your piece of construction paper inside the bottom center of the box with masking tape.

- On the next page carefully pull out or cut out the whole page with the horse picture from the book. From the bottom of the page, cut a line up to the horse. Carefully cut out the horse image and set the horse aside. Don't crumble up the outer paper-this is what you will use for this project. You should be able to see an empty cut-out shape in the middle of the horse paper. Set aside.

- Tape the cut-away part of the horse inside the box, on top of the colored paper. This will work as a stencil.
- Squirt dots of different colored paint the size of a nickel around the edges of the white stencil several times
- Drop several marbles inside the box and roll them around by picking up the box and shifting it around and rolling on top of the paint. You will create a marbled effect shaped like a horse on the paper.
- Let dry. Gently peel off the tape and white cut-out paper.
- Mount the marbled picture on larger construction paper.

Bison Burger Bash for Cash

Chapters 11-12
Birthday Moonflowers & The Clue

Literature Focus - Social Studies

Native American tribes have placed significance on milestones in a child's development rather than the day he or she was born. The day a child takes his first step, takes the responsibilities of an adult, gets married, or becomes a parent is cause for as much rejoicing as the day he was born.

Native Americans celebrate birthdays by choosing a special meal made just for them. Their birthday cake is paraded around for all the guests to see. It is an honor to be asked to cut the cake. Hopi Indians might receive a handmade quilt.

1. What special things does your family enjoy on birthdays?
_____
_____

Discussion Questions

1. What did Jason say his mother did for him on his birthday?
_____
_____

2. Why was Isabel worried that Jason was mad at her?
_____
_____

3. What was Jason looking for?
_____
_____

4. Why was he looking for moonflowers?
_____
_____

5. What happened to Jason's family?
_____
_____

Activity - Make Jason Twofeathers' Moonflower and Morning Glory Teepee

Things you will need:
- Moonflower and Morning Glory seeds: soak them overnight before planting
- 5 or 6 poles about 4 to 5 feet tall
- Strong string or twine
- A patch of ground to build your teepee on

Directions:
- Lay the poles on the ground together.
- Wind the twine around the poles about one foot from one of the ends. Do this 3-4 times then tie it securely.
- Stand the poles up with the tied end on top and spread out the bottom poles to form a teepee.
- Dig up the soil on the outside of the teepee about 2 inches wide and 2 inches deep, except for the area in front that will be the door.
- Pull up any weeds.
- Plant your seeds in the soil about half an inch deep and about two fingers apart. Alternate the Moonflowers and Morning Glory seeds.
- Pat the soil on top so the seeds are covered. Water.
- Water every day and watch the vines grow up the poles.
- Sit under the teepee at night with a flashlight and tell stories like Jason Twofeathers did with his mother.

Chapters 11-12

Vocabulary Words - Crossword Puzzle

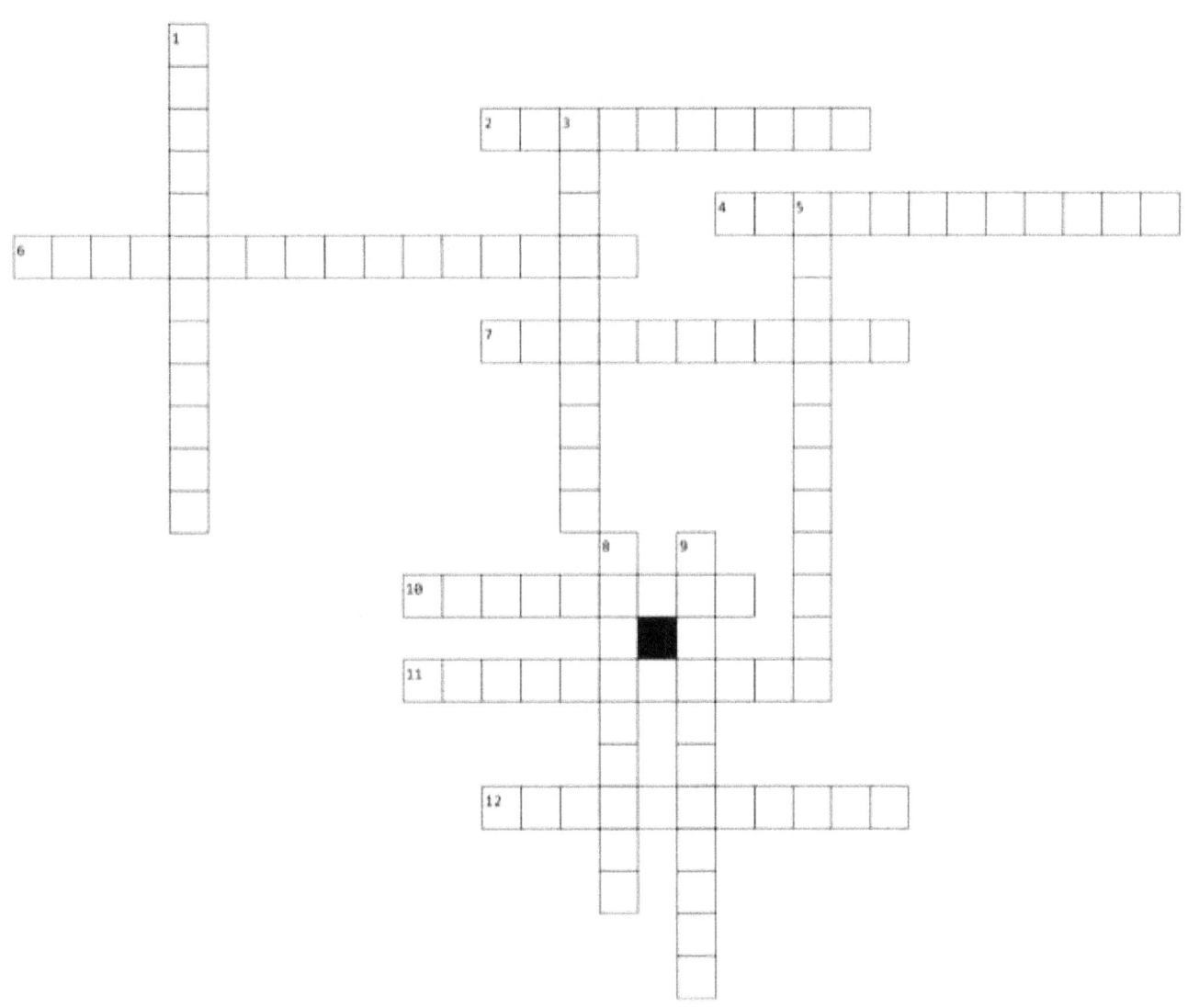

Across

2. being thankful
4. white flowers that reflect the moonlight
6. an oath taken by doctors of proper conduct
7. a group of people born and living during the same time
10. a person who provides a product or service
11. the loss of all hope
12. related to horse riding

Down

1. surrounding and conditions where a person or plant lives
3. made in the original way
5. set of circumstances that makes it possible to do something
8. act exactly like something else
9. produce ideas in a impulsive way

Chapters 13-14
Ms. Morgan's & Bison Burger Bash for Cash

Social Studies Focus

The buffalo was an important animal to early Native Americans. They believed that the buffalo was a generous animal to provide them with food and shelter. The buffalo provided meat for food, and skins for clothing. Large skins were sewn together to make tent walls and roofs for teepees, and horns and bones were used for tools. The Plains Indians had more than 150 different uses for the bison including a water jug from the bladder.

There were 30-75 million buffalo in the early 1800s. Today there are only 550,000 bison in the U.S.

Discussion Questions

1. Why was the plant, Salvation Jane so problematic?
_____

2. What do horses eat and drink when they are on the trail?
_____
_____

3. Have you ever held a Fun Fair? Tell about it. If not, what kind of fair would you like to attend?
_____
_____
_____

4. Isabel chose buffalo burgers for the event staying with the Native American theme. Have you ever eaten a buffalo burger? If so, did you like it? If not, would you like to try one? _____

Activity-Raise Money for Charity

Can you think of a way to raise money for your favorite charity like Isabel and Holly? Some good charities to raise money for are food pantries, mission trips, and Christmas Angel Tree.

Choose a Charity _____

Ideas:

- Sell something you can make.
- Get others involved to help.
- Host a bake sale or garage sale.
- Have yard clean-up days to earn money.
- Do chores for money or donations.
- Get local businesses involved.

Write your ideas here:

_____
_____
_____
_____
_____
_____
_____
_____
_____
_____
_____

Chapters 13-14 Vocabulary Words

Context Vocabulary Game

Instructions: Place the correct vocabulary word or phrase into the blank space in the sentence that matches best. Below is the list of words to choose from.

Words List:

donations	fishy
bash	equestrian
horsemanship	revocation
grant money	perpetually
deadline	caldron
megaphone	rummaged

1. Isabel _____ around in her room looking for her phone.

2. Mom had to finish her cooking for the catering _____.

3. The hot _____ bubbled up at the crab boil.

4. Holly was _____ making videos.

5. The man spoke into the _____ at the circus.

6. Izzy loved having a Fourth of July _____ on her front lawn.

7. Jay received _____ to go to college.

8. The horse whisperer displayed skills in _____.

9. Isabel loved to ride horses at the _____ center.

10. Holly thought something seemed _____ when they found the paper bag at the creek.

11. Mom asked the businesses in town if they would make _____ to help support the burger bash.

Chapters 15-16
Sabotage & A Wild Ride

Literature Focus- Show don't Tell

C.S. Lewis, the author of *The Lion, the Witch, and the Wardrobe* once said, "Don't tell me your characters are afraid but show me in such a way that the hairs on the back of my neck stand up." This is a popular literary technique called "show don't tell". It's using the characters' body language to show what they are feeling instead of telling us.

In this chapter, it is used many times! On the lines below write out how Isabel is feeling.

1. Page 149: Isabel's heart pounded" What was Isabel feeling?

_____

2. Page 149: "Holly gulped and nodded" What was Holly feeling?

_____

3. Page 146: "A group of boys popped up and raced to the corral." What was the author showing?

_____

4. Page 146: "He wrinkled his nose" What was the man showing?

_____

5. Page: 152: "Isabel's lip quivered when she got cockleburs in her hair. What did her actions show? _____

Discussion Questions

1. To sabotage means to obstruct or stop something from happening. What act of sabotage happened in this chapter?
_____
_____

2. Who was the criminal? Did you guess?
_____
_____

3. What tipped Isabel off about who the criminal was?
_____

4. How did Isabel chase the criminal?
_____

5. How did Isabel continue chasing the criminal?
_____
_____

Vocabulary Words – Look up the definitions and write them out below.

SABOTAGE –
_____
_____

SMOKE SIGNAL –
_____
_____

BISON
_____
_____

EMERGENCY –
_____
_____

CONFUSED –
_____
_____

GRANT MONEY –
_____
_____

REPUTATION –
_____
_____

COCKLEBURS –
_____
_____

Activity – Trace the horse on the next page onto a piece plain white paper. Using the magazine mosaic technique – tear out different colored pictures from magazines in the size of dimes, nickels, and quarters. Using a glue stick, glue them on the horse picture side by side touching or even overlapping.

If your horse is brown, tear out many brown pictures from the magazine ripping them into little pieces. All the sides of the squares will be jagged. Do not cut with scissors.

Use white magazine pieces for the white areas, and black for the mane, tail, and hooves. Overlap the pieces or tear pieces into smaller ones to make them fit. Cover the entire horse with magazine pieces.

Use pieces about this size:

About the Author

When Jan May was a little girl one of her favorite times of the year was helping out and attending funfairs with her family. She would wake up early in the morning to help her dad set up booths like the penny toss or the balloon dart games.

Jan is the author of the New Millennium Girl mid-grade novels for girls *Isabel's Secret, Callie's Contest of Courage,* and interactive writing books, *Writing with Isabel, Knights and Castles, Damsels and Dragons, Princess and Frog Fairytale Writing Adventures,* and *Ocean Adventures in Writing.* During her fifteen years as a creative writing teacher, she discovered that given the right tools, any child could write and love it!

New Millennium Girl Books is dedicated to producing wholesome books that inspire vibrant faith in God. Visit us!

Isabel Writing Bundle-A Delightful Language Experience!
"*Creative Writing Made Easy* with *Isabel's Closet* and *Isabel's Secret* literally rocked our world. I have been struggling to teach my daughter to write. I knew she had the heart of a storyteller, but I could not seem to help her to get all her stories on paper. Hand her a piece of paper and she would freeze, cry, and fight her way through each assignment. Until we found this series. It transformed writing time from a terror into a delight!" ~Amy Blevins, homeschool mom and owner at Homeschool Copy work

Other New Millennium Girl books:
Callie's Contest of Courage and Study Guide.

Isabel's Fun Fair Fiasco Study Guide Answer Key

Chapters 1-2

Literature Focus

1. Grrr

2. Thud

3. Poof

Social Studies Focus

1,2,5 Answers will vary

3. Powwow exhibition with Jason Twofeathers

4. Isabel chased after the runaway horse

Chapters 3-4

Discussion Questions

1. They knitted mittens and scarves and sent them food like Holly's cookies.
2. Deer
3. They invited her in to eat.

Chapters 5-6 Literature Focus

Spring Fling Wing Ding

Banana Bandana Punch

Pink Pony Palace

Bison Burger Bash for Cash

Cripple Creek

Discussion Questions

1. To introduce Mom's new catering business to potential customers so they could raise money for the ranch

2. Horse Training on the Ranch

3. Cake pops

4. No, Amanda Parkington was always making Isabel miserable

5. Benjamin Spotted Eagle. He believed in treating horses with kindness and respect. He taught how others to understand horses.

Chapters 7-8 Answers to Crossword Puzzle

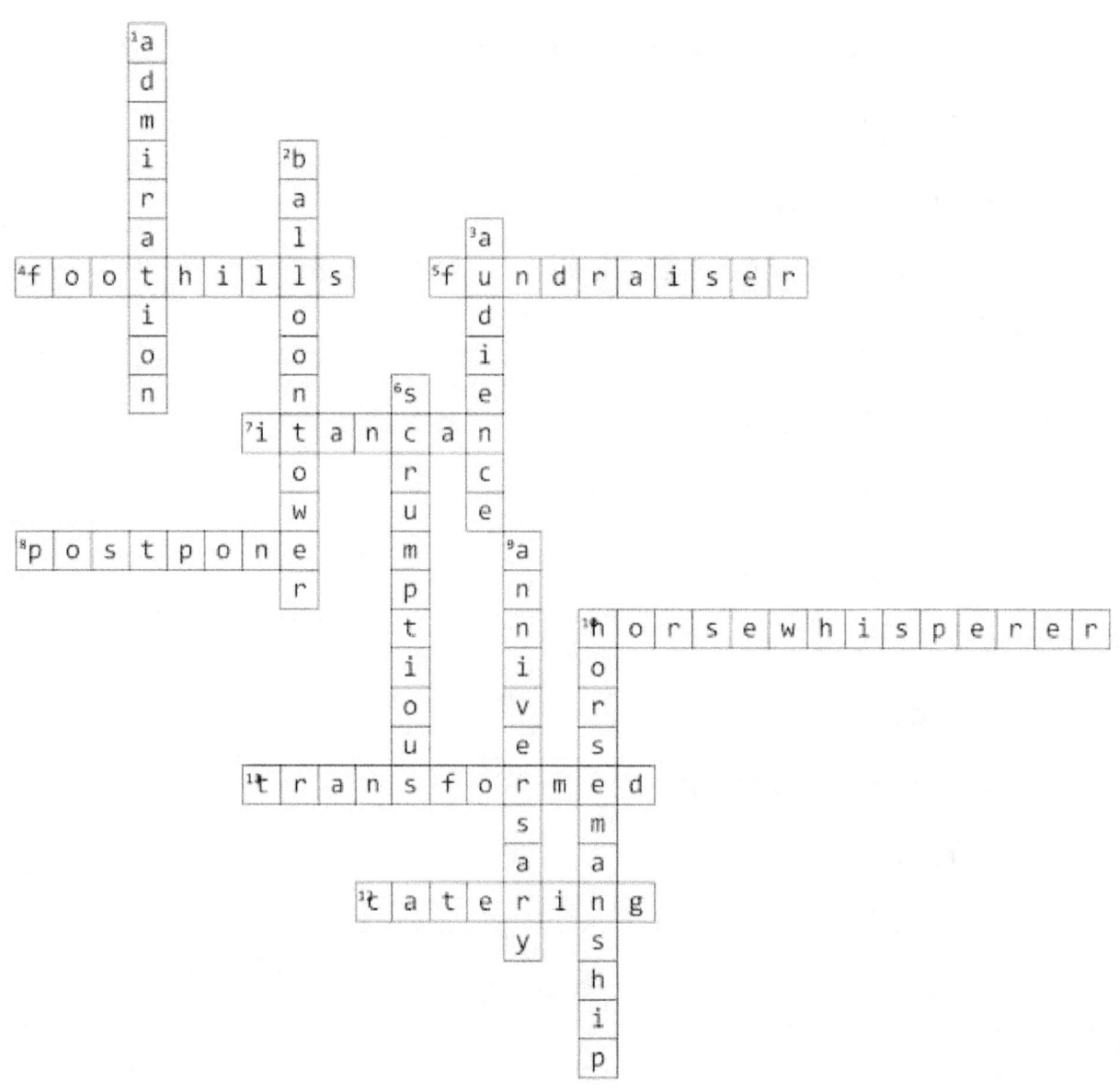

Literature Focus

a thunderstorm

a slithering snake after its prey

a flock of geese

she brought the dark clouds with her in her suitcase

Discussion Questions

1. He said their names pointed to their destiny. Do you agree? Why or why not?

2. Plant Radish seeds in Isabel's name outlined in the dirt.

3. Amanda always tries to annoy Isabel and ruin her life.

4. Gran

5. A poisonous plant

Words in Context Sentences

1. Saddlebag
2. Demonstration
3. Compliment
4. Chauffeur
5. Patterson's Curse
6. Destiny
7. Emerged
8. Limousine
9. Vigorous

Chapters 9-10

Literature Focus

1. The horses were poisoned

2. Isabel

3. Answers below

Suspects	Motives
Gran	Doesn't like Native Americans
Bo	Don't have one yet
Amanda	She's likes to be mean
Doc Harper	Don't have one yet

Clues

Chunky Nutter candy bar wrapper

Dead Bird

Dead Fish

Weather - Rainy and Dark

Discussion Questions

1. A candy bar wrapper

2. Because he had the same candy bar in his pocket.

3. To the Pink Pony Palace. Because it was Amanda's house.

5. That Jason was mad at her and blamed her for poisoning the horses.

Chapters 9-10 Word Search Answers

```
. . . . D . . I . . . . . . . . S . D
. . . . S E . N . . . . . . . U G E
. . R . C L V V . . . . . . P S A M
. S E . R O . E . . . . . . E P R O
. U V . U A . S L . . . . . R I G N
. S O . T T . T . O . . . . S C A S
. P L . I H . I . . P . . . U I N T
. E T . N S . G . . . M . . A O T R
. C I . I O . A . . . . E . D U U A
. T N . Z M . T . . . . . N E S A T
. . G . E E . E . . . . . . T . N E
S Y M P A T H E T I C . . . . . . .
```

Chapters 11-12

Discussion Questions

1. Planted a moonflower teepee and told him how proud she was of him.

2. Because the horses got sick.

3. Moonflowers.

4. Because it was his birthday.

5. His father turned bitter and mean then went missing for 3 days. His boots were found on the riverbank. People think he fell in and drown. His mother died from tuberculosis 2 years previous.

Chapters 11-12 Crossword Puzzle

Chapters 13-14

Discussion Questions

1. It was poisonous

2. They drink from the brook and eat grasses and plants

Context Vocabulary Sentences

1. Rummaged
2. Deadline
3. Caldron
4. Perpetually
5. Microphone
6. Bash
7. Grant money
8. Horsemanship
9. Equestrian
10. Fishy
11. Donations

Chapters 15-16

Literature Focus Questions

1. She was nervous and afraid

2. She was worried

3. They were in a hurry to be first.

4. He didn't like the taste of the burger.

5. She was hurt and wanted to cry.

Discussion Questions

1. Someone changed the bison meat for liver and put itching powder in the face paint.

2. Skeet Savage

3. Skeet Savage was coming out of her house with a suspicious grin and a red shirt with a missing button. Then she overheard him talking to the principal who admitted everything

4. On horseback but she fell off

5. Jason scooped her up as he was riding Thunder